Mallorca

The island of a thousand faces

Mallorca

The island of a thousand faces

Text

ALBERT HERRANZ

TRIANGLE POSTALS

Contents

Mallorca

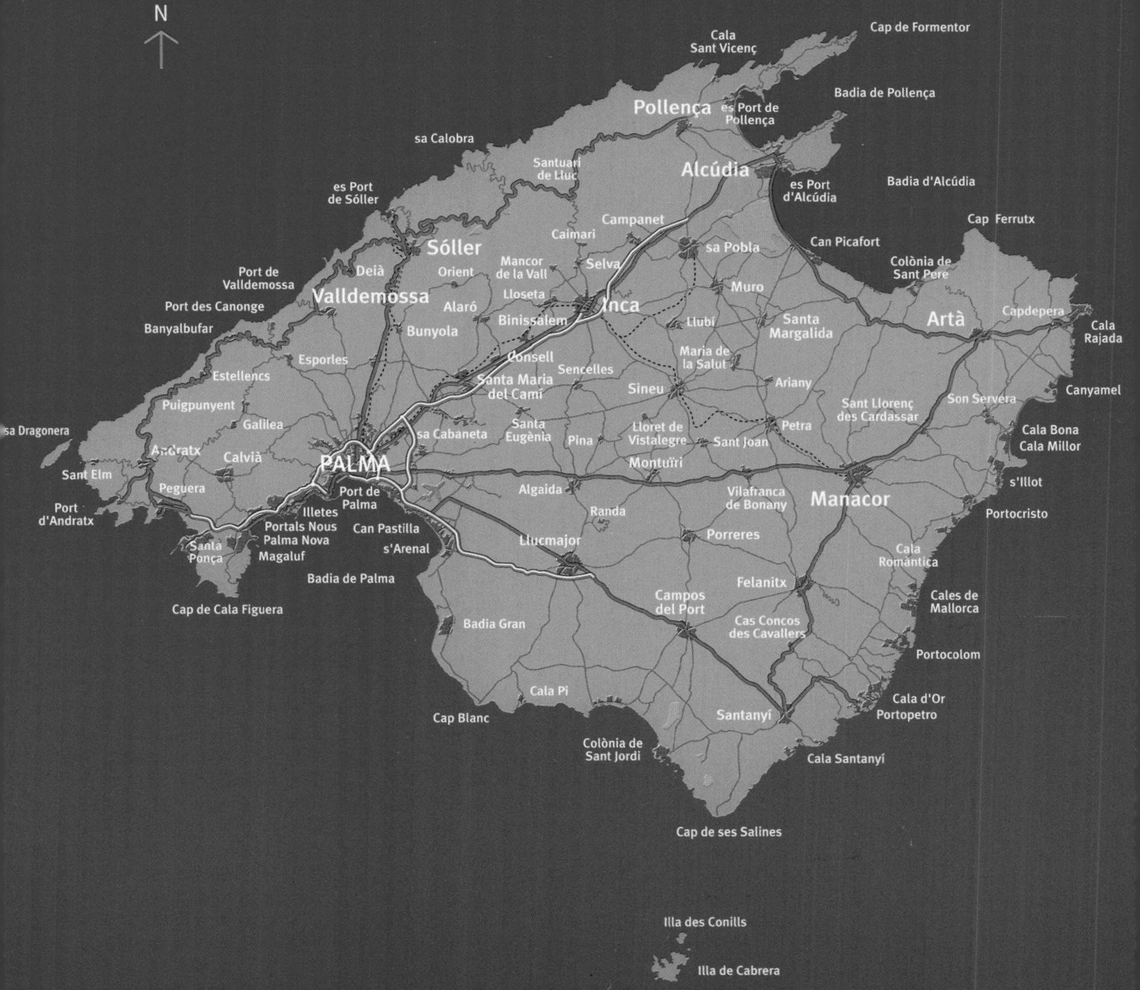
N
Cap de Formentor
Cala
Sant Vicenç
Badia de Pollença
Pollença
es Port de
Pollença
sa Calobra
Santuari
de Lluc
Alcúdia
es Port
d'Alcúdia
Badia d'Alcúdia
es Port
de Sóller
Campanet
Cap Ferrutx
Caimari
Can Picafort
Sóller
sa Pobla
Colònia de
Sant Pere
Port de
Valldemossa
Deià
Orient
Mancor
de la Vall
Selva
Muro
Valldemossa
Lloseta
Inca
Port des Canonge
Alaró
Artà
Capdepera
Binissalem
Llubí
Santa
Margalida
Cala
Rajada
Banyalbufar
Bunyola
Esporles
Consell
Maria de
la Salut
Estellencs
Santa Maria
del Camí
Sencelles
Ariany
Son Servera
Canyamel
Sineu
Sant Llorenç
des Cardassar
Puigpunyent
Galilea
Santa
Eugènia
Lloret de
Vistalegre
Petra
Cala Bona
sa Dragonera
sa Cabaneta
Cala Millor
Andratx
Calvià
Pina
Sant Joan
PALMA
Montuïri
Sant Elm
Peguera
Algaida
s'Illot
Port de
Palma
Vilafranca
de Bonany
Manacor
Port
d'Andratx
Illetes
Randa
Portocristo
Portals Nous
Can Pastilla
Palma Nova
Porreres
Santa
Ponça
s'Arenal
Llucmajor
Cala
Romàntica
Magaluf
Badia de Palma
Felanitx
Cales de
Mallorca
Cap de Cala Figuera
Campos
del Port
Cas Concos
des Cavallers
Badia Gran
Portocolom
Cala Pi
Cala d'Or
Portopetro
Cap Blanc
Santanyí
Colònia de
Sant Jordi
Cala Santanyí
Cap de ses Salines
Illa des Conills
Illa de Cabrera

Mallorca is the most well known western Mediterranean island in the world. In how many languages has its name been pronounced in? In how many languages have dreams been woven alongside the beaches of Cala Rajada or Cala Figuera? Who has not followed the coastline with their eyes from Sant Elm and come across the sleeping shadow of the island of Sa Dragonera? Who has not felt, with a slight shiver, echoes of pirates and corsairs at the foot of the ports of Sóller, Andratx or Pollença? Mallorca is the island where characters from marvellous tales passed from generation to generation live alongside real personalities who belong to a fashionable world of popular legend. Giants, film stars, dragons, lucky millionaires... varied geography, a source of surprises, an unending supply of questions for the curious traveller, or a treasure island for the anxious tourist in search of sensations... Mallorca is a contradictory island: here the past and present live alongside each other. Beneath the lazy trained vines or the bustling beaches it is difficult to define the personality of this esteemed island: it possesses a diverse and captivating personality.

The island of a thousand faces

Mallorca is a mosaic of innumerable colours that form its geographic and human territory. In the embrace of the Mediterranean, it awaits the visitor patiently.

In just 3,640 km^2 its inhabitants jealously guard a millennial world full of Arab reminiscences, of traces left by discrete travellers throughout history, echoes of periods of fear and swords, the illumination of wise men such as Ramon Llull who wanted to unite the three cultures that have marked this blue Mediterranean within a universal peace. Nevertheless, the Mallorcan people are, despite this zeal, an affable and tolerant people.

The interior seems to make out the foaming sea that surrounds *la roqueta* and the coast drifts off with the fragrances of the orchard, the humid land of the interior. A land of tranquil farming folk, of brave sailors, of craggy coastlines in the north and friendly beaches in its bays –Palma and Alcúdia– it sometimes seems to be snoozing beneath the midday sun. Let us not be taken in by appearances: under the golden cloak of the sun the activity stirs. Mallorca is no stranger to adopting modern methods, in trying out new formulas, befitting its history as a land of bold merchants. Despite its ironic tone, the sunlit wisdom, fruit of the hundred-year-old olive tree, means that it maintains a sceptical view of modernity. With the same strength from which it adapts, it abandons. This island reserve means that the past and the present live alongside each other here. This reserve, maybe even mistrust, enables Mallorca to be

Springtime fills the fields with colour

a mosaic of strong contrasts. Each of the pieces cries out to be discovered, known, enjoyed like the fragrance of orange blossom or the slow passing of summer days.

This mosaic of contrasts was a secret shared by travellers and adventurers in bygone centuries, until in the nineteen-fifties the secret was revealed to the world. Mallorca was the leader of a tourist boom upon which, today, a certain limit has been placed. Deigning a type of development befitting other periods, Mallorca is seeking out and trying new ways to protect and care for its land: natural parks, protection for unspoilt beaches... in this way we can go trekking, dance in furiously modern venues, wander around curious churches and museums, enjoy its beaches to the full, sit ourselves down in a *celler* (bodega) and taste its unknown wines or simply take in the twilight while treating ourselves to a delicious dish of fresh fish... As a child of distinct sensibilities, Mallorca has equal attraction for those who prefer programmed visits and for those who prefer spontaneity and adventure.

The old "possessions" are a valuable heritage

The island's main attraction is its coastline

I

Palma de Mallorca
Calvià
Andratx
Valldemossa
Deià

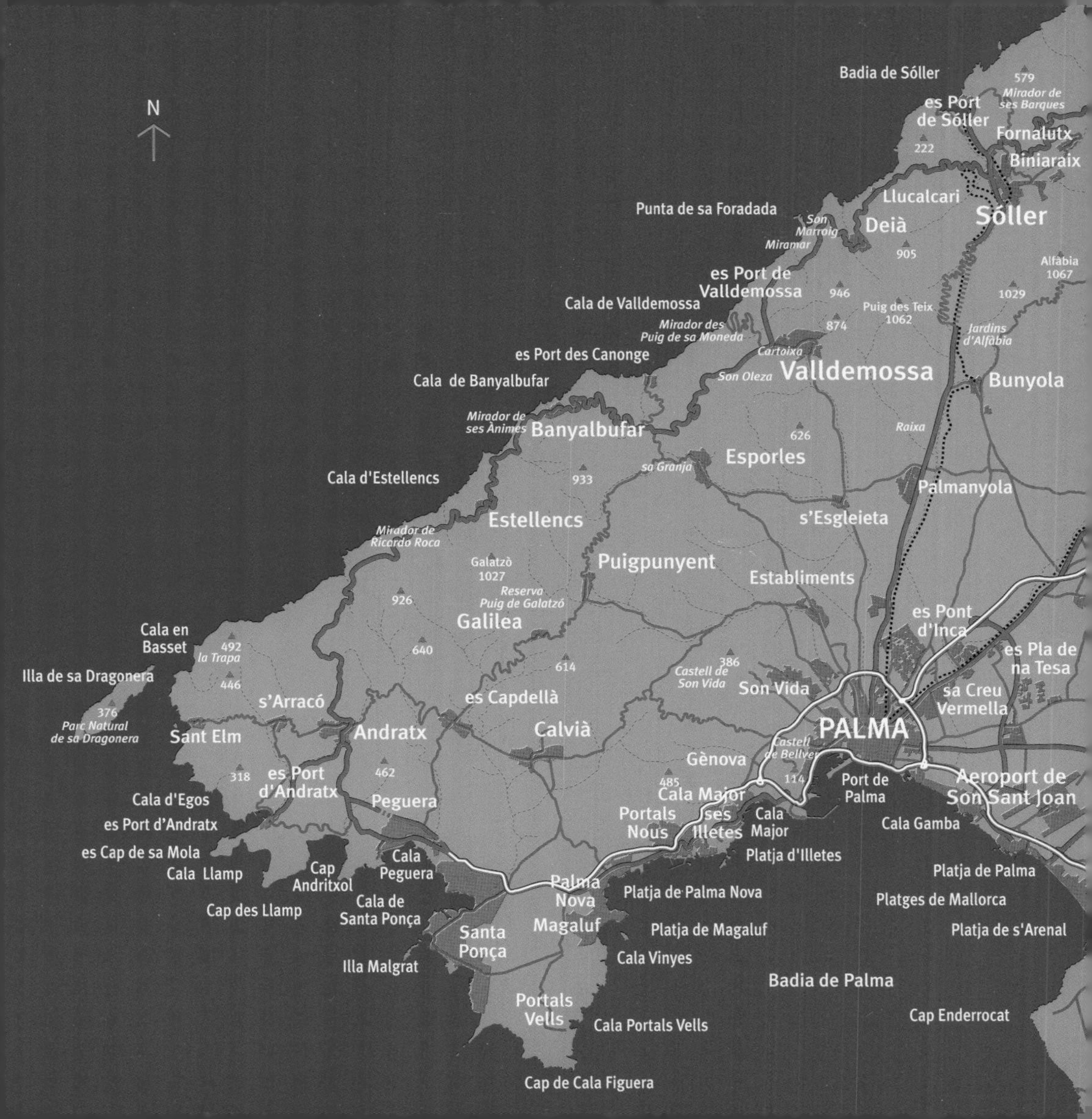
N
Badia de Sóller
579
Mirador de ses Barques
es Port de Sóller
Fornalutx
222
Biniaraix
Llucalcari
Sóller
Punta de sa Foradada
Son Marroig
Deià
Miramar
905
Alfàbia 1067
es Port de Valldemossa
946
Puig des Teix 1062
1029
Cala de Valldemossa
Mirador des Puig de sa Moneda
874
Jardins d'Alfàbia
es Port des Canonge
Cartoixa
Cala de Banyalbufar
Son Oleza
Valldemossa
Bunyola
Mirador de ses Ànimes
Banyalbufar
Raixa
626
Esporles
sa Granja
Cala d'Estellencs
933
Palmanyola
Estellencs
s'Esgleieta
Mirador de Ricardo Roca
Puigpunyent
Galatzò 1027
Establiments
Reserva Puig de Galatzó
926
es Pont d'Inca
Galilea
Cala en Basset
492
la Trapa
640
es Pla de na Tesa
386
614
Castell de Son Vida
Illa de sa Dragonera
446
Son Vida
sa Creu Vermella
s'Arracó
es Capdellà
376
Parc Natural de sa Dragonera
PALMA
Sant Elm
Andratx
Calvià
Castell de Bellver
Gènova
318
es Port d'Andratx
462
485
114
Port de Palma
Aeroport de Son Sant Joan
Cala d'Egos
Cala Major
Peguera
Portals Nous
ses Illetes
Cala Major
es Port d'Andratx
Cala Gamba
es Cap de sa Mola
Cala Peguera
Platja d'Illetes
Cala Llamp
Cap Andritxol
Palma Nova
Platja de Palma
Platja de Palma Nova
Cala de Santa Ponça
Platges de Mallorca
Cap des Llamp
Magaluf
Platja de Magaluf
Platja de s'Arenal
Santa Ponça
Illa Malgrat
Cala Vinyes
Badia de Palma
Portals Vells
Cap Enderrocat
Cala Portals Vells
Cap de Cala Figuera

Palma de Mallorca

Capital of the island. The first city up to the point of being named thus by the Mallorcans: simply *Ciutat* (City). Due to the influence of the Italian Renaissance, it recovered its ancient Roman name during that period, Palma, and the double name survives to this day. Gate of departure, a valued bridge for the islanders to the outside world, it is also a news centre, a place of arrivals, of meeting up with the world that from here sometimes seems so far away...

The bay of Palma was highly valued in ancient times and that led to the Romans founding a colonial settlement here. Later on, after the passing through of Vandals and Byzantines, the Arabs enlarged it and turned it into the beautiful orchard that led Jaume I the Conqueror to state with admiration that Medina Mayurqa was the most beautiful city he had ever set his eyes on. Ciutat saw the passing of kings and merchants laden with gold coins and fantastic tales, until it was the turn of another illustrious visitor, Charles V, to stand before the walls of the city in admiration. And the centuries pass as time moves on, leaving their mark on this millennial city, ancient Roman settlement, ancient capital of a kingdom and today a European centre par excellence.

Whether one arrives by sea or by air the urban profile of two buildings stand out: La Seu (the cathedral) and the Castle of Bellver.

La Seu dominates the bay and is the building that best sums up Palma. With a rectangular ground plan and three naves, it not only possesses impressive examples of Gothic and Baroque art but also

The magnificent cathedral overlooks a cosmopolitan port

guards inside a monumental votive lamp, the work of the architect Antoni Gaudí and a decorated chapel, still in the process of creation, entrusted to the internationally known Mallorcan painter Miquel Barceló. Centuries of Mallorcan art have contributed to this collective work that is La Seu. Alongside it stands the Palau de la Almudaina, an old palace of the Mallorcan monarchs, a Muslim and Christian mixture of medieval art, which today is where the Spanish monarchs are received when making official visits. Beneath these two monuments the Parc de la Mar stretches out, a park in which the people of Palma wander around, enjoy concerts and other leisure activities while watching the reflection of the cathedral in the water of its beautiful lake.

An apprentice in the cathedral, the architect Guillem Sagrera designed Sa Llotja, a beautiful building of slender columns that along with the Consolat del Mar, the current headquarters of the local government, are two witnesses carved in stone of the importance that the sea has had for the city. Sick and tired of the unreliability of his

Large entrances enhance the stately homes

Entrance courtyard to Can Vivot

countrymen when it was time to pay Guillem Sagrera left for Naples. It is no coincidence that the relationship with Italy is a close one in many aspects, evidence of which can be seen in the wide, open Gothic courtyards of the old quarter: Can Oleza, Can Oleo, Can Catlar, Can Berga, Can Morei... the Castle of Bellver, where from whose walls we can take in the view of the whole bay and the city, also noting the relationship in its circular ground plan.

We can divide old Palma according to the old names of Canamunt and Canavall (the upper and lower parts), which have their boundaries on either side of the old course of the Sa Riera stream. The old quarter is the part of the city that hides the most treasures: the innumerable churches (Santa Eulària, Sant Jaume, Monti-sion...), the Gothic cloister of Sant Antoniet, the Arab Baths, the hidden courtyards... and in the city's nerve centre, Cort (the council) with its renaissance facade, the Palau del Consell with a neo-Gothic facade, and beyond the Plaça Major, always bustling with craftsmen and street performers, the modernism of the Gran Hotel, Can Casasayas,

The interior of the Seu is highlighted by the baldaquin designed by Gaudí

The spires of the cathedral, seen from the Palau March

"El Águila", Can Corbella, Can Forteza Rey... Also worthy of a visit are the districts of Es Molinar, El Terreno and Santa Catalina. El Terreno was once a residential area, as can be seen from the opulent houses in which unmistakable artists such as Rubén Darío, Gertrude Stein, Camilo José Cela, Rusiñol and Albert Vigoleis sought refuge and lived.

The districts of Es Molinar and Santa Catalina, in contrast, have more humble origins and possess a marked seafaring character, and in either area one can enjoy the rich island gastronomy.

Other attractions of Palma include the numerous art galleries and cultural centres (Misericòrdia, Flassaders, Sa Nostra, Grand Hotel...) which mark the cultural beat of the city. A little further out from the centre is the Fundació Joan Miró, which provides the visitor with a complete series of interesting activities and works of Joan Miró, the painter who loved this island so much. We can also delve into the ever-changing nighttimes on the outskirts of Sa Llotja, Gomila or the sports port that occupies the central part of the bay.

Casa Forteza Rey

Modernist baker's

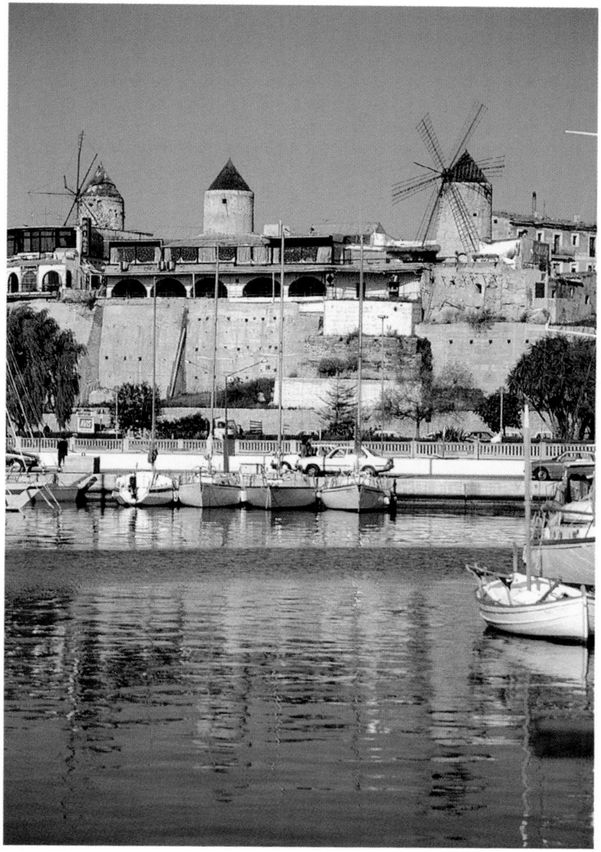

Windmill in the Palma district of Es Jonquet

← Fireworks above the Parc de la Mar

Palau March, headquarters for the museum of the Fundació Bartolomé March

La Llotja, one of Palma's most symbolic buildings →

The castle of Bellver overlooks Palma from a hill
← By walking around the old quarter the visitor discovers the city's past
The strange mills of Pla de Sant Jordi →→

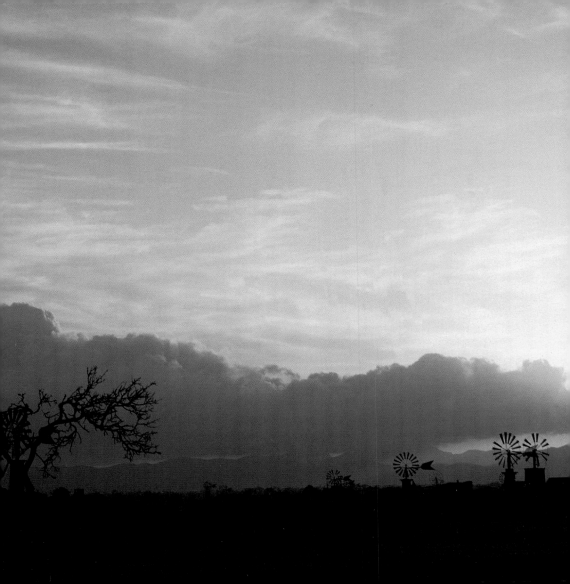

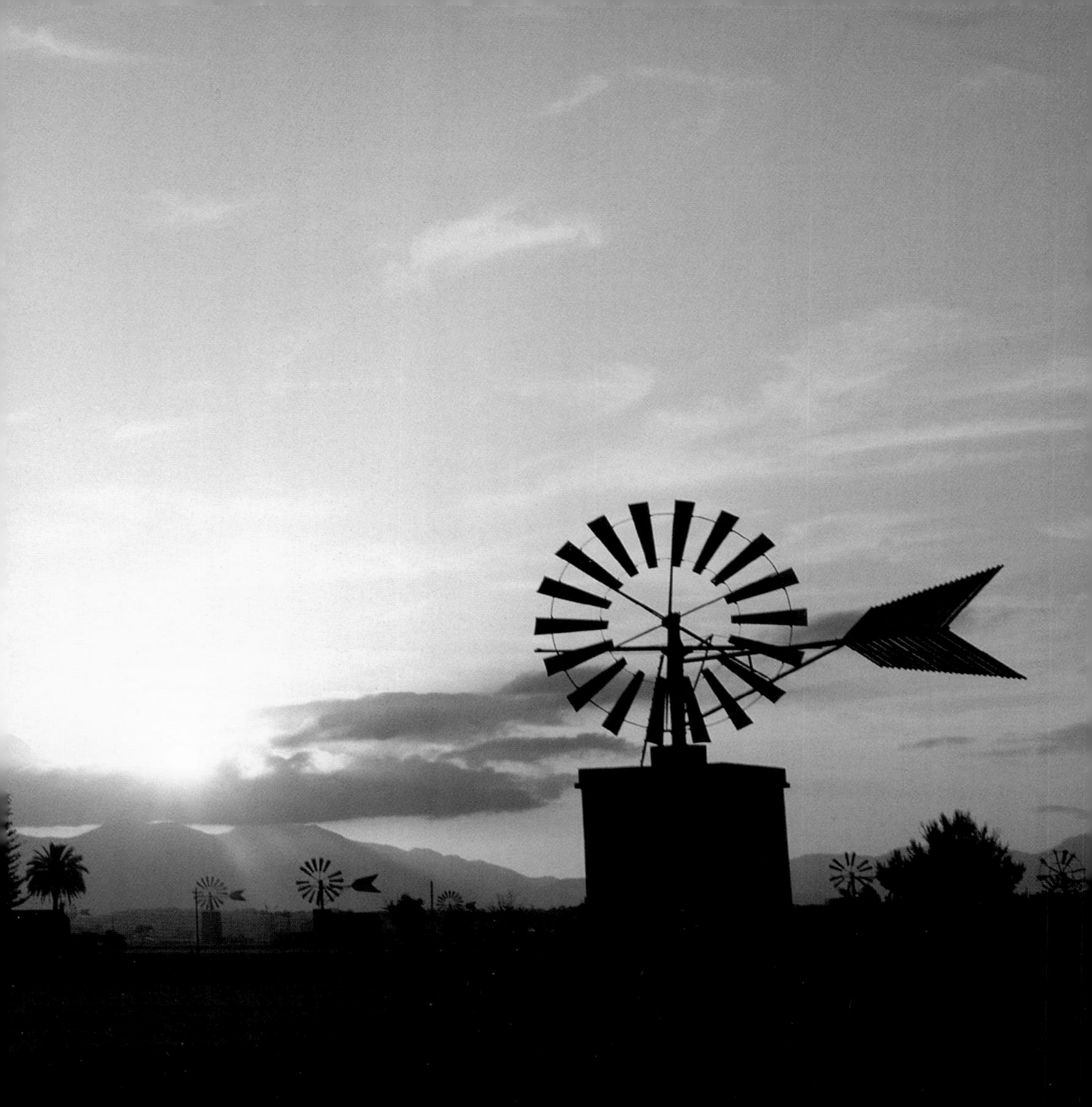

Portals Nous

Portals Nous is the small Nice or Monaco of Mallorca. Its exclusive sports port is the refuge and playground of the famous figures that visit the island. If you want to know what next year's fashions will be, look at these personalities or simply enjoy a chic atmosphere, then Portals Nous is an obvious choice.

This corner, of a markedly leisure-based and elitist nature, is in the town of Calvià, between Bendinat and Costa d'en Blanes. Until the beginning of the Civil War it was the spot where many middle class families had their second home. At the end of the 1950s the first hotel was opened and today around the port there are six hotels, eleven bars and some ten restaurants in Portals Nous. It is worth underlining that in 1986 the sports port was founded, with 670 moorings, and the Sailing Club, with around 500 students each summer.

Cala Portals Nous, with the En Sales islet

The sports port

attraction

Magaluf

Magaluf, also located within the rich municipality of Calvià, the pioneer in tourism in Mallorca, is perhaps the corner of the island that has suffereded most urban aggression. Nevertheless, it is also the first area that has been seen to benefit from the new sensitivity that the Mallorcan tourist industry has developed. A traditional leisure-spot of the English, part of the fashions and trends in music that later set the pace in Great Britain have their origins in Magaluf. As well as the traditional tourist fare, Magaluf provides new experiences more in line with the respect for nature. With extensive beaches surrounded by a beautiful boulevard, it is gradually recovering its lost charm.

From its coastline we can begin to make out the mountainous north of Mallorca.

Magaluf's main beach

Twilight over the sea

Santa Ponça

E al cessar que féu lo vent veem la yla de Maylorque. (And when the wind died down we saw the island of Mallorca) recounts king Jaume I in his chronicles of the conquest of the island. The pleasant coastline of Santa Ponça was the setting for the landing of Christian troops as its inhabitants recall each year with a dramatised recreation and proclamation that always emphasises the positive aspects represented by a mixture of cultures. Santa Ponça has been a much-visited land as is shown by the numerous prehistoric excavations, ruins of Punic trading posts. The charms of Santa Ponça are not only its beaches: here you can also develop your love for golf at the Golf Club of Santa Ponça, where the Balearic Open is held, or make the most of other sports facilities (a pelota court, tennis courts, football pitch, etc.) or take part in the regattas of the Nautical Club of Santa Ponça.

Es Malgrat islets

General view of Santa Ponça

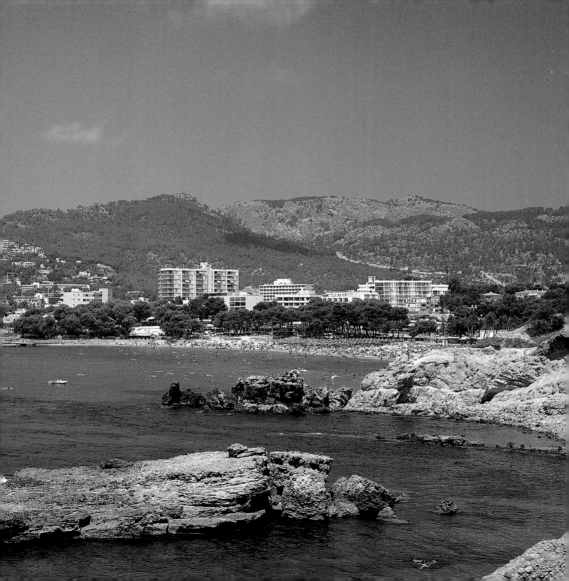

Peguera

Peguera is a very new centre though it does not appear so, development having begun in 1958. However, there are documents showing the existence of a pitch (*pega grega*) workshop in the 15th century, and it is this activity that its name seems to come from. Today, despite the focus on tourism, it still preserves examples of a fruitful agricultural past that led to, at the end of the 19th century, the export of large quantities of capers to France.

In Peguera, if you are of a curious nature, you can combine the beach with rambling. You should also remember that leading painters such as Francisco Bernareggi, Pedro Blanes and Antoni Gelabert also stayed in this privileged spot.

Punta des Carabiners, with Peguera in the background

Es Racó de ses Llises, in Cala Fornells

Es Cap de sa Mola, facing the Sa Dragonera isle
El Camp de Mar, coastal development close to Andratx →

Andratx

Andratx is a dynamic town that until the 14th century lived with its back to the sea due to the frequent attacks by Berber pirates. Later it became a town of fishermen and farmers. Andratx, which today survives mainly from tourism, is one of the most legendary towns on the island: amongst its narrow streets and wide avenues are hidden tales of smugglers, pirates, mercenaries, or emigrants who got rich in America or died in poverty. Andratx is a low mountain town: it is not closed off into a single valley but extends along several valleys of almonds orchards and wheat.

A visit to the church and the Castle of Son Mas, currently the home of the Town Council, is an absolute must. Andratx is also known for its craftsmanship in the production of ropes, due to the abundance of *garballó* (palm heart). Next to Andratx is the small

Andratx, at the foot of the Serra de Tramuntana

Castillo de Son Mas, the Town Hall

village of S'Arracó. For nature lovers there are several interesting natural areas, such as Cap des Llamp or Cap d'Andritxol where you can see a varied wildlife such as hedgehogs, rabbits and genets. The outlet of the Saulet stream is also another interesting spot with one of the few stable populations of green toad, endemic sub-species of Mallorca.

Its port stands out with its beautiful canal and the moored fishermen's boats. Andratx is a high-class tourist centre. To the east of the port is the Mola d'Andratx, a small peninsula joined by a narrow strip of land from which the island of Sa Dragonera can be made out.

Outlet of the Torrent des Saulet

The Puig de Galatzó overlooks the valley and the port's waters →→

Seafront of Port d'Andratx

Sant Elm

In the old fishermen's village, Sa Dragonera is omnipresent. This islet, which many compare with a sleeping dragon –in Catalan, *dragó*– is home to lizards and is a Natural Park due to its wealth of marine birds and birds of prey, its rich seabed and the fact that the threat of development awoke the consciences of the Mallorcans, giving rise to a state-wide movement in favour of protecting the islet. One could say that this is where the ecology movement in Spain was born. From Sant Elm the islet can be visited by taking a public transport boat with an extensive timetable. Sa Trapa is at 400 metres altitude and in an impressive landscape of cliffs dominated by the ruins of a Trappist monastery. Worth mentioning are the 14 species or orchids to be found here. The old watchtower and the white sand of the beach of Sant Elm justify a visit in themselves.

Es Pantaleu islet, facing Sa Dragonera

Cala en Basset, a hard-to-reach but pleasant corner

The isle of Sa Dragonera from the viewpoint of La Trapa
Examples of the flora and fauna present in the Natural Park →

Estellencs

It is a small village, both in physical and human terms: some three hundred inhabitants live there. It is enclosed in the valley and surrounded by mountains: Moleta de S'Esclop (900 metres), Sierra de Pinotells (730 m), Penyal del Moro (618 m), Moleta Rasa (681 m), Serra dels Puntals (882 m) and without forgetting the foreboding shadow of the mountain of Galatzó (1,027 m). From the village you can make different excursions around the surrounding mountains or bathe in the port located some distance away. A constant view, due to the past threat of pirates, is of the district's defensive towers. Coming from Andratx an obligatory stop-off is Es Grau, with its viewpoint dedicated to the engineer Ricard Roca and from which you can see an imposing view of the craggy northern coast.

Winter setting

The village, sheltered by the Mola de Planícia

Banyalbufar

Just like Estellencs, Banyalbufar is a mountain village, overlooking the sea from its height of 100 metres. Although it is not as closed-off as Estellencs, the landscape of crops on terraces or *marges* is the same. Their name comes from the Arabic *bunjola al-bahar,* which means "small vine of the sea": it was famous for its wine in Roman times, and continued to be so until the plague of phylloxera that hit Mallorca finished off the crops. The speciality of Banyalbufar, malmsey wine, was produced again after decades of neglect, and is delicious even for the most demanding of palates.

The village's culture is closely linked to water: the many water mills and the *ma'jil,* the system of water distribution introduced by the Muslims are clear evidence of this. Also, in the village centre stands the Torre de la Baronia.

The houses are built on the staggered terraces

Inside courtyard of the Torre de la Baronia

Watchtower in the Mirador de ses Ànimes

View towards the west from the same viewpoint →

Valldemossa

Valldemossa may well be the most well known village in Mallorca. Illustrious visitors such as Jovellanos, George Sand, Chopin or Rubén Darío have been responsible for putting the village on the map. The omnipresent shadow of Chopin and George Sand is cast over the old Carthusian convent, La Cartoixa. The famous couple spent time in the village in 1838-39, leaving behind them a rich assortment of anecdotes and gossip. George Sand wrote a book about her Mallorcan experience, *A winter in Mallorca*, which is a classic work about the island. In each home in the village we can

The Sant Bartomeu tower sticks out over the rooftops

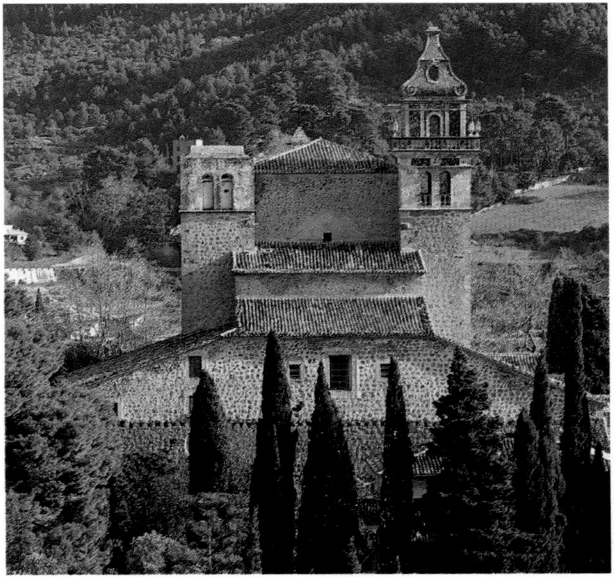

La Cartoixa is home to a grand cultural heritage

come across a glazed tile of the most venerated saint in Mallorca, Saint Catherine Thomas. A native of the village, the house where she was born is still preserved today. Nevertheless, Valldemossa has more things to offer: from its rich potato *coca* (sweet pastry) through to a pleasant stroll around its adorned and narrow cobbled streets. Five kilometres away is Miramar. It was once the residence of the Archduke of Austria Ludwig Salvator, author of an encyclopaedic work, *Die Balearen*, about the Balearic Isles. It was also in Miramar where Nicolau de Calafat set up the first printing press in Mallorca and where Ramon Llull founded his school of translators of oriental languages (1276). We should also mention Son Marroig, which houses a museum dedicated to the Archduke, the Hermitage, the Port de Valldemossa and the 13th century village church. Some famous visitors have left their mark on the village, as is the case of the actor Michael Douglas who created the Costa Nord centre where you can enjoy a good meal and attend concerts or other cultural events.

Flowers and cobblestones in the Carrer de sa Rectoria

Valldemossa, between the parish church and La Cartoixa →→

Feline relaxation

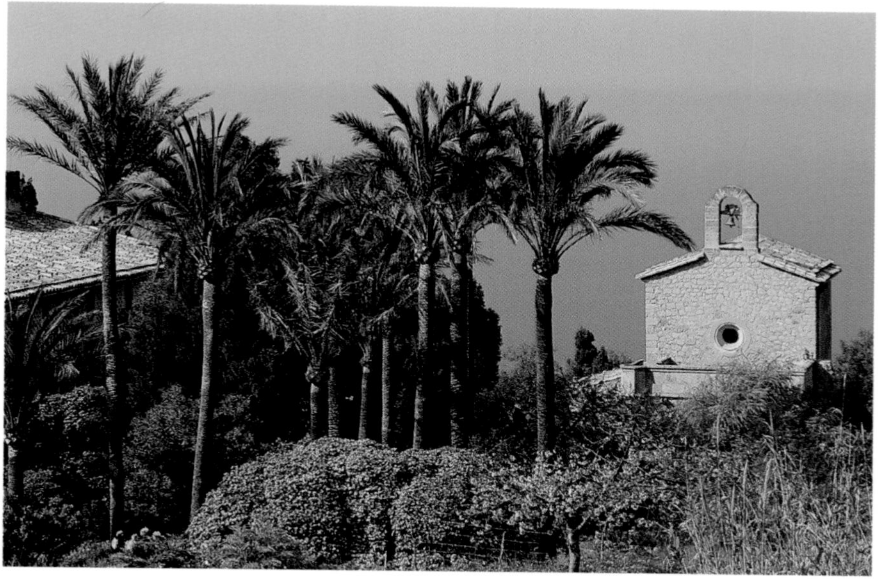

Hermitage of Miramar

← From Miramar you can see the tip of Sa Foradada

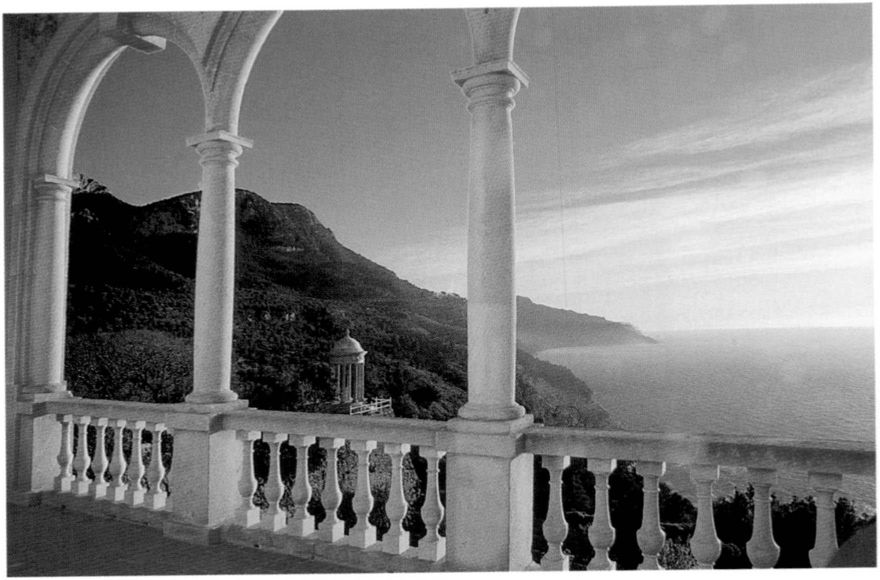

Son Marroig gallery

View against the light in Sa Foradada →

Deià

The village is located on a hill in the shadows of the Teix mountain (1,062 metres). Its outstanding feature is the stone houses that climb up the steep slope until reaching the church and cemetery. It is raised in a point like the bow of a ship towards the sky and the sea.

The origin of Deià is Muslim and this can be noted in the layout of its streets and the irrigation system, still in use. The village is the centre of a constant flow of famous visitors. It is quite common to see famous singers and musicians performing in one or other of the village's bars. The outskirts of the village are ideal for rambling: there are paths that connect with the neighbouring villages (Sóller and Valldemossa). Half an hour's walk away –it can also be reached by car– is Cala Deià, whose crystalline waters are famous. Among the long list of illustrious

The stone houses cover the hill

The early evening light highlights the spectacular scenery

visitors feature the well-known English poet and novelist Robert Graves (author of *I, Claudius, The White Goddess...*) whose remains rest in the cemetery. From the time he arrived in the 1920s, he fought for the preservation of the village, and his presence there attracted a large group of intellectuals of different origins. Deià has its own Archaeological Museum, Parish Museum, the museum in honour of the painter Norman Yanukin and the International Festival of Deià.

Also worthy of mention are the series of houses in Llucalcari, next to Deià, as well as the Cala de Es Canyeret some fifteen minutes from the village where naturism is possible. In the cove is a stony area with a spout from which fresh water flows from the mountain range and a clay-like mud, used by some for mud baths. Alongside this cove are others that can be reached without any difficulty whatsoever.

Llucalcari with the tip of Sa Pedrissa in the background

Fishermen's cottages grouped together in Cala Deià

The cormorant swims and fishes in this limpid pool
← The inlet boasts calm waters for anchoring

2

Sóller
Lluc
Pollença
Formentor

N
Cap de Catalunya
Cap de Formentor
334
Cala Sant Vicenç
Cala Sant Vicenç
Castell del Rei
542
350
Cala Pi de la Posada
el Port de Pollença
Cap des Pinar
Ternelles 839
Badia de Pollença
Cala de sa Calobra
el Calvari
Pont romà
Pollença
Platja des Coll Baix
Cala Tuent
Puig de Maria 333
445
Puig Roig 1002
Alcúdia
462
Torrent de Pareis
1103
es Port d'Alcúdia
Escorca
443
247
Illa d'Alcanada
Monestir de Lluc
s Port Sóller
268
Badia d'Alcúdia
579
Puig Major 1447
Mirador de ses Barques
Emb.des Gorg Blau
Massanella 1352
327
Platges de Mallorca
532
Coves de Campanet
Fornalutx
Binibona
Campanet
Ullaro
ses bassetes 1216
Parc Natural de s'Albufera
Embassament de Cúber
1047
Platja de Santa Margarida
Caimari
Biniaraix
sa Pobla
Can Picafort
Sóller
l'Ofre 1091
Mancor de la Vall
Moscari
Selva
Búger
Necròpolis de Son Real
Alfàbia 1067
Biniamar
Inca
s'Alcadena 813
Muro
1029
Orient
Lloseta
Puig d'Inca 307
Jardins d'Alfàbia
Alaró
Binissalem
Santa Margalida
671
Bunyola
Llubí
Santa Maria del Camí
Jornets
Maria de la Salut
Palmanyola
Biniagual
Consell
Costitx

Gardens of Raixa, on the road from Palma to Sóller
← *Gardens of Alfàbia, at the entrance of the Sóller Tunnel*

Sóller

Until recently separated from the rest of the island by the mountainous barrier of the range and, with the railway and a winding path –Coll de Sóller– as the only means of access, Sóller developed an individual idiosyncrasy that led it to establish close commercial and social links, still in force, with France. Its rich modernist houses (Can Pruna, Banc Central Hispano, the Gran Via street...), the tram and the selfsame railway tell us of a city that was an important capital for the textile industry and exporter of citric fruits. Today access by car has been made easier with the construction of a toll motorway, though it is well worth entering the town aboard the Tren de Sóller, an electric railway that, since 1912, with its wooden, cast iron and glass wagons, passes through twelve tunnels which, in a zigzag, go around the valley of the town until reaching the terminal station.

Modernist church of Sant Bartomeu

Sóller Botanical Garden

"Moors and Christians" Festival in Port de Sóller
Sóller during the festival, the station and the popular tram →

BILLETES
TICKETS

Gabi
BAR

SERVICIO AGENCIAS
22

The main square, full of terraces and life, is the authentic nerve centre of the town. Here is the Town Council, the neo-classical church of Sant Bartomeu. We can reach the port on the tram, which is 2 km away, and has a series of beaches and a sports port. From the port excursions are organised to distinct parts of the island (Sa Calobra, Na Foradada...). Also of note are the Balearic Museum of Natural Science and its botanical garden. The *Sa Fira* and *Es Firó* festivals are held during the second week of May and feature the traditional battle of Moors and Christians, dances, markets and exhibitions. During July and August the important International Folklore Festival is held with participants from all over the world.

The mountains surrounding Sóller, the citric fruit orchards and the pathways that cross them make up an ideal spot for going on excursions.

The tram connects the town with the port

The train from Palma entering the valley of Sóller

Seafaring atmosphere in the Port de Sóller

View of the port from the Ses Barques viewpoint →

COPA KINDER
COPA ADVOCAT
COPA FRUTA
COPA CARAMELO
ORANGE SOLLER
BANANA SPLIT

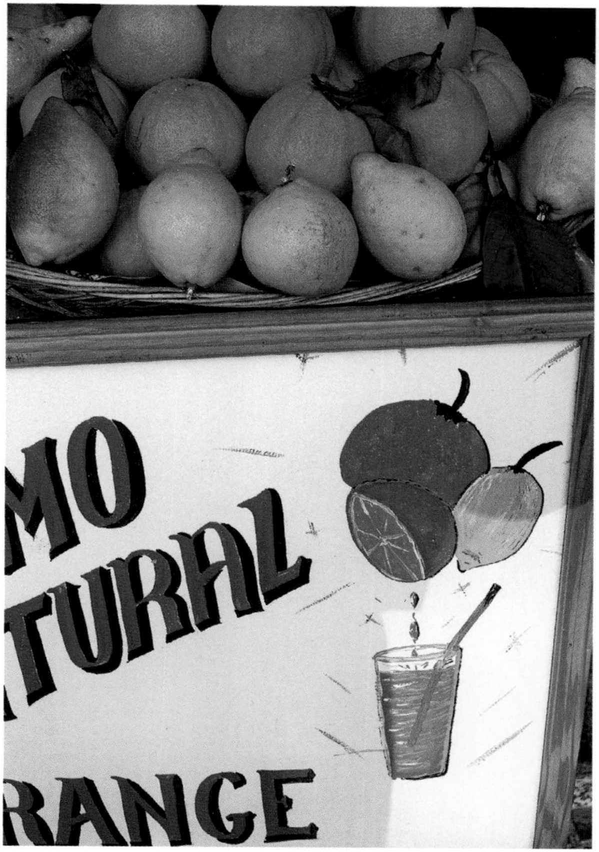

The local citrus fruits are made into ice creams and juices in summer

Biniaraix

This is a small village on the outskirts of Sóller. It is noteworthy for its series of houses and gardens, its terraced streets and the church of Santa Maria (1634). The traditional *Trobada de Pintors del Barranc,* a meeting of painters, is usually held in April. The path known as the Barranc de Biniaraix leads from the village to the entrance of the valley of L'Ofre. It then retraces the Barranc stream and is cobbled. It is an absolute delight, since the path crosses over the stream at constant intervals. The landscape, full of terraces and stone walls, which take on odd shapes following the course of the stream, hide a rich flora and fauna. In the book *Las islas Baleares* (1888) Piferrer states, "By a very narrow and fast-falling slope that winds between precipices, we climb the Barranc exhausted, and stop with amazement to take in the rounded mountains that tower over us, and then continue gazing towards the profundity of the craggy mountainsides".

Streets and houses are adapted to the landscape of the ravine

Rural setting with hundred-year-old olive tree

Fornalutx

Fornalutx is considered to be a remarkable spot of scenic and architectural interest. At 166 metres above sea level, it has always lived in the shadow of Sóller, being an independent district since 1837. There are very interesting houses (Can Arbona, the council building, Casa d'Amunt, Posada de Balitx, Can Xandre, Can Ballester, Can Bisbal...) and the church, with a remarkable organ inside, already documented in 1484. A particular trait of the houses in the village are the painted tiles on the eaves (28 properties counted). This feature is repeated throughout the valley of Sóller.

Springtime smiles out over the town

A terraced street, a garden of multiple fragrances

The mountain architecture forms quite remarkable images
← Interior of the Bàlitx d'Avall country hotel

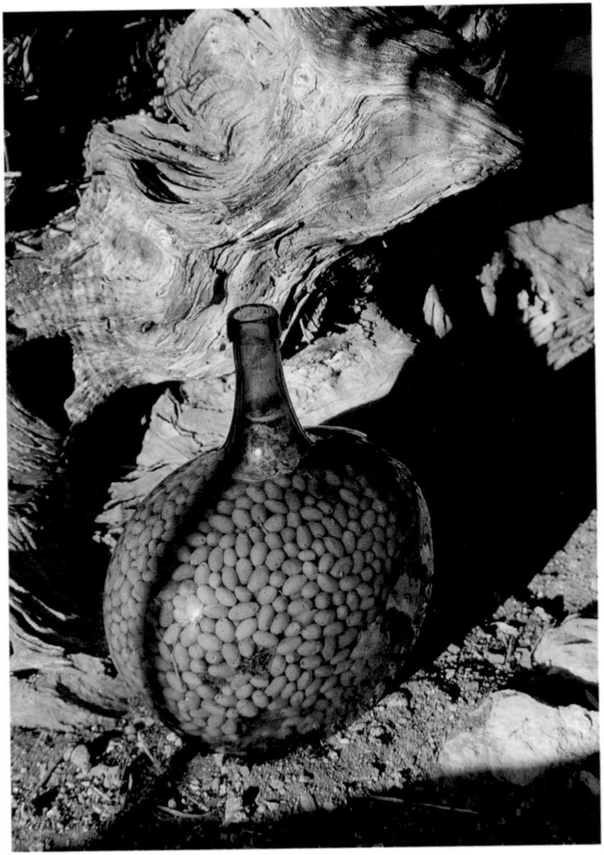

The culture of oil survives on the island

Old mill in the Mofarès oil press →

Sa Calobra

Sa Calobra can be reached by crossing the whole Tramontana range by the road from Sóller to Lluc, reaching the coastline along a winding route, especially designed as a tourist attraction by the engineer Antonio Parieti, or by going along the coast from Port de Sóller by boat, or along the long and sinuous mountain paths.

In fact there are two enclosed coves, surrounded by walls of rock with a very particular physiognomy of crevices and relief. One of the coves, S'Olla, is the outlet for the Torrent de Pareis. It forms an enormous natural amphitheatre where enjoyable choral concerts are often held. At 122 metres above sea level the cove cannot be seen from the exterior. The waterfall is a classic drop in Mallorcan ravine descent.

Sa Calobra belongs to the mountainous district of Escorca, the least populated of the island and ninth largest in size.

Outlet of the Torrent de Pareis

From Sa Calobra you can reach the adjoining cove along a tunnel

The *possessions*, or estates, are the most important urban element (Mortitx, Mortitxet, Mossa, Femenia, Binifaldó, Binimorat, Cúber...). This district includes the mountain peaks of Puig Major (1,447 m), l'Ofre (1,091 m), Puig de Massanella (1,352 m) and Puig de Ses Bassetes (1,216 m) and the most important streams on the range have their sources here: Almadrà, Massanella, Coma Freda... There are around 60 springs and over 30 archaeological sites. Both on the outskirts of Sa Calobra and in Escorca you can go walking, go on longer excursions or go mountaineering, but you should always take great care. Another interesting spot is Cala Tuent, a white, fine sandy beach that is 180 metres long.

The impressive opening ends in a small beach

Cala Tuent beach, neighbour of Sa Calobra

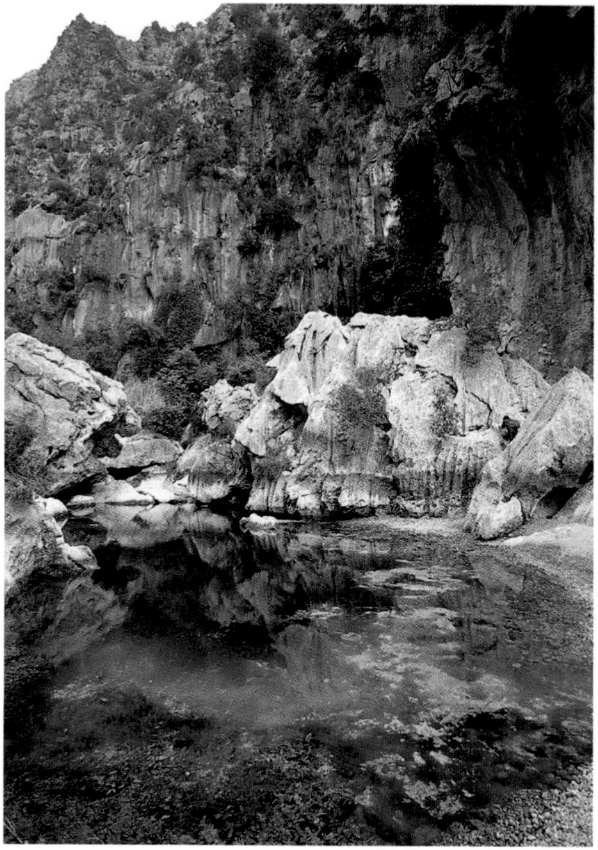

One of the bends in the Torrent de Pareis

← Another view of the interior of the ravine

Sanctuary of Lluc

The sanctuary of Lluc is the spiritual heart of the island – the name comes from the Latin *lucus,* sacred forest – and the patron saint of Mallorca, the Virgin of Lluc, is worshipped here. Her image is made from polychromed stone and is in Gothic style (15th century), and is dressed in the habit of the old owners of Lluc, the Knight Templars. According to the legend she was found by a shepherd alongside the current sacristy shortly after the conquest of the island.

The sanctuary's boys' choir is famous, and are known as Els blauets for the colour of their *blau* (blue) cassocks. It is one of the oldest institutions in Europe (1531) with a long-standing and well-known musical history. There is a museum exhibiting the prehistoric remains of the Cometa dels Morts and the main jewels of the Virgin; and another museum with a botanical garden where many endemic species can be seen. There are also guest quarters for the many pilgrims that arrive here.

Clot d'Albarca with Puig Roig in the background

View of the sanctuary and its environs

Olive trees on the outskirts of Lluc

← Silhouette of Puig Major from the Sa Calobra road

The Fonts Ufanes, a natural phenomenon of this area

Stalagtites and stalagmites in the famous Campanet caves

Cala Sant Vicenç

In contrast to what its name may suggest, Cala Sant Vicenç, 7 km from Pollença, is not one cove but three: Cala Barques, Cala Clara and Cala Molins and several streams have their outlets in them. Sheltered by the Cavall Bernat (the extension of the mountain range that drops to the sea), its waters are calm and transparent, except when a Tramuntana storm stirs them up. There is a small and peaceful tourist resort and the setting arouses a special sensitivity. It is no coincidence that painters such as Anglada Camarasa, Santiago Rusiñol and Sorolla found inspiration for their works here.

Cala Sant Vicenç has also been the focus of different underwater archaeological campaigns and has some of the most important artificial burial chambers of Talayotic culture. The scenery surrounding Cala Sant Vicenç is spectacular and you can make different walking trips or climbs.

Cala Molins, protected by the walls of Cavall Bernat

Cala Barques, forming part of Cala Sant Vicenç

Osprey

Clear waters in a stunning setting →

Pollença

The town centre of Pollença is 4 km from the bay of the same name. The name of Pollença comes from the Latin participle and adjective *pollens*, to have strength, which would define it as the city with drive, with power. It is a peaceful town with a noteworthy central square, adorned with large plane trees and with typical bars, such as Can Moixet (Bar Espanyol). Despite this peacefulness, it was here that Agatha Christie wrote her novel *Problem at Pollença Bay*.

The Roman two-arched bridge, alongside the church, built by the Templars, and the Baroque convent of Sant Domingo, are spots well worth visiting. The Festival of Pollença has been held in the inner courtyard of the convent for the last forty years, a series of concerts of great prestige in Europe. The recurring image of the town is the stairway that begins in Calle Jesús: 365 steps flanked by cypresses and a Way of the Cross with impressive crosses; it

The Calvari Hill

The Plaça Major, in the centre of the town

represents the ascent to the Calvary. At the end of the stairway we come across the oratory and some viewpoints from which the whole of Pollença can be seen. Another privileged vantage point is the Puig de Maria, from where you can see splendid views of the peninsula of Formentor, the bay of Pollença and the valley of Sant Vicenç. The Puig de Maria has a hermitage with rooms for spending the night. The area is rich in plant and bird species. The Castell del Rei is the ruins of the old royal castle of Pollença. Of Muslim origin and situated at 476 metres altitude its ruins overlook part of the district, The castle, finally abandoned in 1732, was given its first stage of rehabilitation between 1992-94.

One of the most popular festivals on the island is held in Pollença: the Representation, or traditional battle between Moors and Christians, dedicated to the town's patron saint, the Virgin of the Angels. In the Representation, the *pollencins*, the locals, celebrate the victory in 1550 over Turkish pirates. The two sides are led by two historical characters: the pirate Dragut and the

The locals, the "pollencins", take their festivals very seriously indeed

Cloister of the Baroque convent of Sant Domingo

Moixet
CA

mayor Joan Mas, played by local inhabitants elected from a strictly organised election.

The local gastronomy boasts the *formatjada*, a rich cottage cheese cake. In the district there are several rustic style furniture factories and in the city there are several shops specialising in decoration and gift articles. The outdoor market is in the town on Sundays and in Port de Pollença on Wednesdays.

Between Pollença and Alcúdia is the Area of Special Interest of S'Albufera, the first natural reserve of Mallorca.

Albercutx beach, in the Port de Pollença

The range of El Morral d'en Font protects the port

The bay of Pollença preserves corners of an idyllic beauty

Seafront promenade. In the distance you can see the Formentor road →

Formentor

The most impressive scenery in the district of Pollença is undoubtedly found on the protected peninsula of Formentor with its cliffs, rugged mountains that rise majestically to fall heavily into the ever-changing sea. A winding road that crosses the peninsula follows the numerous cliffs. It ends at the Far de Formentor, a spot of dramatic beauty that rises gently to two hundred meters above sea level, and from where you can make various trips to many coves (Cala Murta, Cala Boquer, Cala Figuera...) or watch the fascinating birds that nest in the area.

At the beginning of the twentieth century, two millionaire Argentine artists appeared in Pollença, Adan Diehl, a writer, and Roberto Ramaugé, a painter. The latter, who fell in love with the scenery, built the famous Hotel Formentor in Cala Pi. The legendary hotel has an elegant terrace and graceful gardens.

Punta de la Nau and the islet of El Colomer, seen from the viewpoint

Early evening against the light

Famous figures of the last century such as Grace Kelly, Winston Churchill, Rainier of Monaco and the Duke of Windsor were guests here. It has also been the setting for meetings between world-famous writers responsible for the awarding of the Biblioteca Breve International Prizes, or of influential politicians at different world summits. At the foot of the hotel is the Platja de Formentor, a beach of white sand surrounded by a dense pine forest.

The Hotel Formentor was the setting in which the strange word "estraperlo" was invented, a combination of the names of two Dutch businessmen, Strauss and Perle, who thought up a new roulette game that was set up in the hotel and in the casino in San Sebastián. In exchange for allowing its introduction, the head of the government, Lerroux, would receive part of the profits. The governor of San Sebastián banned the game and when Strauss appealed to Lerroux, the latter washed his hands of the matter. The scandal finally hit the headlines, the roulette wheels were removed and Lerroux resigned. The word has become synonymous with the term black market.

The lighthouse caps the craggy cape of Formentor

The peninsula is the northernmost point of the island →→

From Cala Pi you can make out Puig de la Pinoa

3

Alcúdia
Natural Park of s'Albufera
Artà
Capdepera
Portocristo

Badia de Pollença
Cap des Pinar
Platja des Coll Baix
sa Talia 445
Pollentia
Teatre Romà
Alcúdia
247
es Port d'Alcúdia
Illa d'Alcanada
268
N
Platges de Mallorca
Parc Natural de s'Albufera
Badia d'Alcúdia
Cap Ferrutx
432
Can Picafort
444
Cala Matzocs
Cala Estreta
Cala Mitjana
Cala Mesquida
Muro
Necròpolis de Son Real
es Figueral de Son Real
Cala des Camps
Betlem
Ermita de Betlem
562
405
Cap des Freu
271
Cala Moltó
Cala Agulla
Son Serra de Marina
sa Colònia de Sant Pere
Puig de Ferrutx 522
Castell de Capdepera
Cala Rajada
Punta de Capdepera
Cala Rajada
Santa Margalida
Artà
Sant Salvador
Capdepera
Cala des Carregador
Font de sa Cala
Cala de sa Font
487
ses Païsses
Maria de la Salut
sa Torre de Canyamel
204
Coves d'Artà
Ariany
Costa de Canyamel
Platges de Canyamel
472
Son Servera
Costa des Pins
Cap des Pinar
Sant Llorenç des Cardassar
Platja des Ribell
Petra
Cala Bona
Cala Bona
Badia de Son Servera
nt Joan
Cala Millor
Cala Millor
Son Carrió
Vilafranca de Bonany
Manacor
Cala sa Nau
Castell de N'Amer
Punta de n'Amer
sa Coma
Platja de sa Coma
s'Illot
s'Illot
Cala Morlanda
Cova dels Hams
300
Portocristo
Coves del Drac
Son Macià
Cala Anguila

Alcúdia

Alcúdia is one of the towns in Mallorca that takes most care of its historical and cultural heritage. This is confirmed by a stroll through its old quarter, cobbled and with single-storey houses or two-storey at most, surrounded by a well-preserved wall. The walled city deserves some serious visiting: here can be found the Porta de Xara, surrounded by gardens, and the Porta de Sant Sebastià (also called the Porta de Mallorca).

Alcúdia houses the ruins of the Roman city of Pollentia, founded in 123 BC by the Roman coloniser of Mallorca, Caecilius Metellus. The city, preserved and with several culturally-orientated routes, is completed with an amphitheatre. With the fall of the Roman Empire the city was assailed by the Vandals and finally became a farmstead under the domain of the "taifa" kingdom of Dènia. The town's name comes from this period: Alcúdia means hill.

Porta de Xara, vestige of the old walls

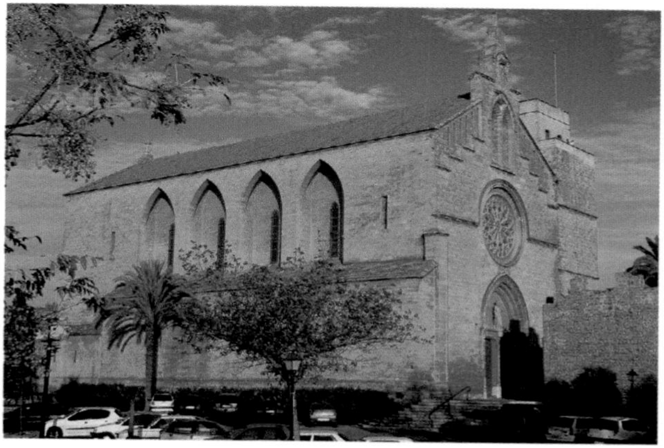

Parish church

Mallorca becoming part of the Kingdom of Aragon dates the beginning of the construction of the walls, which acted as protection for the noblemen and large estate owners during the rising of the *Agermanats,* brotherhood of peasants. These events resulted in it being awarded the title of "Loyal City" by Charles V. A victim of constant attacks and pillaging by corsairs and pirates, the population of Alcúdia progressively decreased until, in the 18th century, a process of resettlement began.

Although the main source of local income is now tourism, it should be pointed out that the town has an important industrial base, thanks partly to the presence of the port and the power station that supplies electricity to Mallorca and Menorca, the island with which it has a regular sea connection. Fishing is also another well-rooted activity.

Port d'Alcúdia

Port d'Alcúdia, as well as its long seafront, has a beautiful and lengthy beach with shallow water. Other beaches include Mal Pas and Ses Caletes, both facing the bay of Pollença, and S'Alcanada,

Long beaches to enjoy the sun and the sea

nearby the port and protected by a small island with a lighthouse with the same name. Another natural asset is the marshy land of S'Albufera, a Natural park and an absolute paradise for ornithologists.

Alcúdia is home to the Fundació Can Torró, a library equipped with the most modern reading methods and which organises all kinds of cultural activities; it was donated to the town by one of the most important publishers in Europe, Reinhard Mohn (Editorial Beltersman). The Fundació Yannick i Ben Jakober is located in a remarkable building, by Hassan Fathy.

Gateway of Sant Sebastià, or Mallorca, in the Alcúdia wall →→

Ruins of the Roman city of Pollentia

Roman amphitheatre

Ses Caletes, at the eastern end of the bay of Pollença

Es Coll Baix beach, at the foot of Sa Talaia d'Alcúdia →

Example of the purple heron
← S'Albufera is a unique natural space

The Park enables you to observe protected species.
Many birds inhabit or reside seasonally in S'Albufera →

Can Picafort

Located at the end of the bay of Alcúdia, Can Picafort is a dense series of property developments and hotels that occupies a lengthy stretch of coast between the road and the sea with sand dunes that go from the beaches of Santa Margalida and Muro to the Cala de S'Aigo Dolça. The beaches have fine sand and the seafront is very pleasant. You can go by bike to Port d'Alcúdia, covering 10 km, the scenery is flat and nearly the entire way can be done on a cycle path. The water here is not as calm and shallow as in Alcúdia. Close to the sea there are a lot of typical hotels that are mixed up with the facades of the residential houses. The entire seafront is scattered with bars and restaurants where you eat while resting your eyes watching the waves rolling in and drifting out.

Wihtin the area we also find the impressive Talayotic necropolis of Son Real, on the public estate of the same name.

Santa Margarida beach

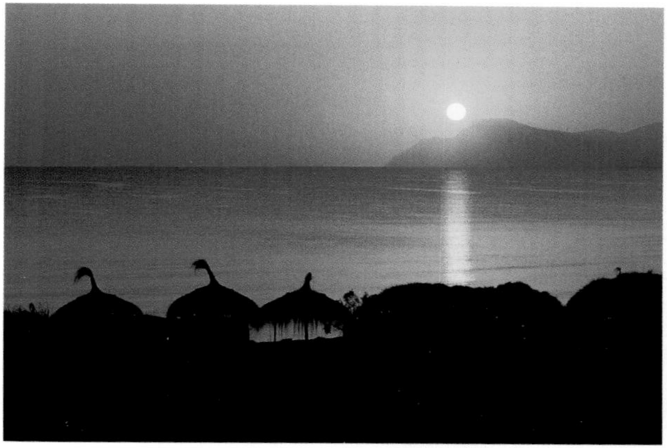

Sunrise in the bay of Alcúdia

Colònia de Sant Pere

The parcelling-off of the agricultural estate of Farrutx in 1880 led to the creation of the coastal town of Colònia de Sant Pere. Colònia has been the traditional summer resort for the *artanencs* (the locals from Artà). Another spot with a particularly Mallorcan atmosphere is Son Serra de Marina, which regularly plays host to the *murers, inquers, margalidans,* and *poblers,* residents, respectively, of Muro, Inca, Santa Margalida and Sa Pobla.

A popular excursion consists of going to Cap Ferrutx on foot. The path passes by pleasant coves such as Caló des Camps or Es Canons.

Corner of Es Caló, close to Cap Ferrutx

Beach in Colònia de Sant Pere

The "rupit" (robin), one of the species that inhabit the area

← The almond tree blossom lights up the landscape

Artà

The origins of Artà have been lost in the mists of time. The ruins of the Talayot de Ses Païsses, which can be visited, bear witness to this. During Roman times, it seems that it was an important enclave, and in the Muslim period the district formed one of the thirteen parts into which the island was divided. With the conquest of Mallorca by Jaume I the current town of Artà was founded.

Important agricultural activity and textile production gave rise an increase in the number of inhabitants. The bubonic plague, however, decimated the population in 1820 and many people also emigrated to America.

Tourism first took hold in the nineteen-sixties, revolutionising the building and leisure sectors in the area. Nevertheless, in Artà there is also agriculture, livestock breeding and some food industries.

Sanctuary of Sant Salvador

Turret in the wall of Artà

In the old quarter feature the buildings of the *indianos*, the emigrants who returned from the Americas as wealthy people (Can Sureda, Cas Marqués, Can Cardaix...) and the castle-cum-hermitage Santuari de Sant Salvador. The sanctuary is reached by a stairway of 180 steps that start off from the church. During the plague of 1820 it was used as a hospital, and even though it had been built in the 14th century, the building was burnt down and rebuilt as a result of the plague. A pleasant excursion takes us to the hermitage of Betlem, from where we can see the whole bay of Alcúdia. There is a series of peaceful coves, such as Estreta and Mitjana.

One of the town's big celebrations with deeply-rooted traditions is the festival-saint's day balls of Saint Anthony, which takes place on the 16th and 17th of January.

Cala Estreta and Cala Mitjana, on the peninsula of Artà

Cap des Freu

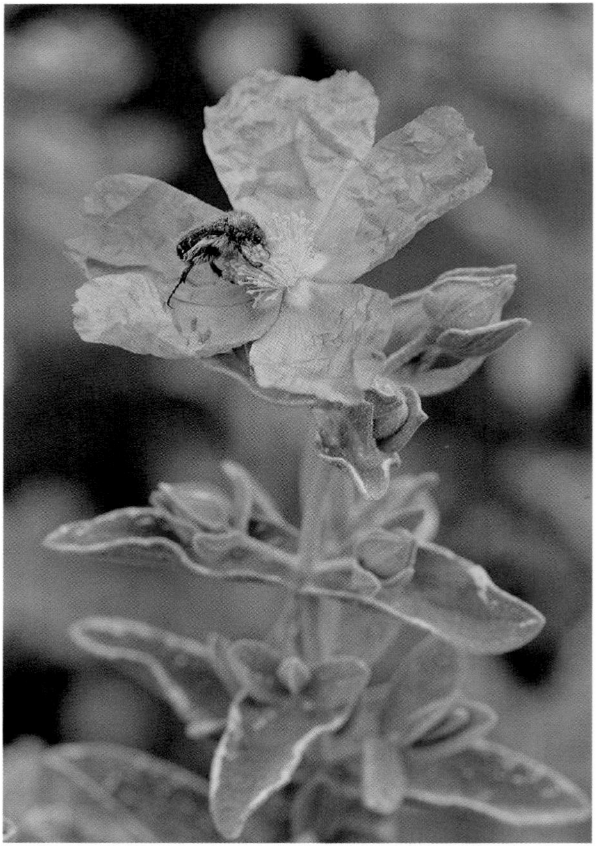

The Halimium halimifolium, rockrose, a delicate flower in the middle of barren land

The parsnip is another species that resists this rugged environment →

Capdepera

Just 8 km from Artà, Capdepera was originally its patrol point towards the sea. Jaume II ordered the construction of a villa on a hill that was at 162 metres above sea level. For centuries Capdepera survived enclosed in its walls and defence towers against pirate attacks. As the danger of these attacks disappeared, the inhabitants gradually left the villa to settle at the foot of the hill. The old villa is now called Castell de Capdepera. At the top of the walled precinct is the oratory of Nostra Senyora de l'Esperança.

On the coastline, the beaches and coves of Cala Gat, Cala Agulla, Cala Moltó, Es Carregador, Cala Lliteres... and two islets: Es Freu, alongside the cape of the same name, and Faralló, at the entrance of Cala Gat, are important features. For a long period of time it was commonly known as Far de Capdepera as a simile of a distant or inhospitable place.

The castle walls crown the town

Cala Mesquida and Coll de Marina in the background

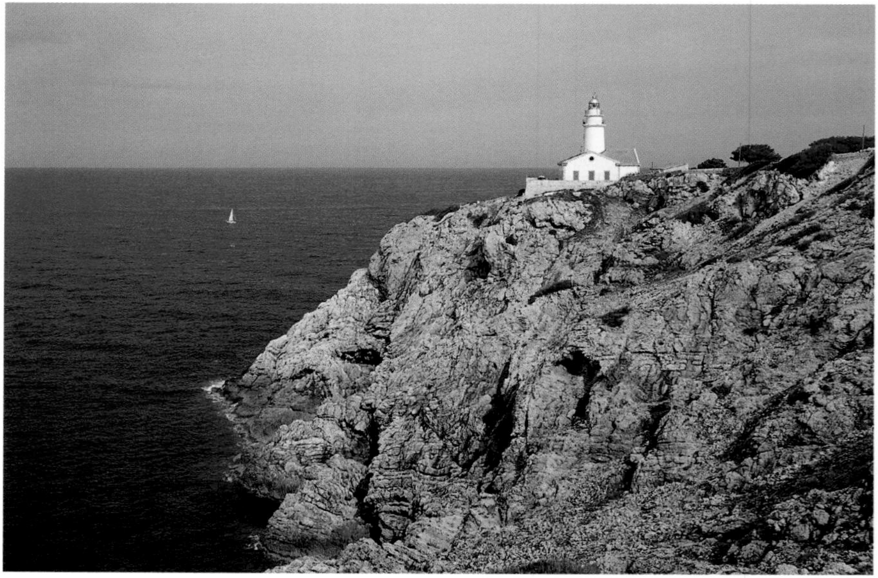

Lighthouse on the rocky spot of Punta de Capdepera

Cala Agulla and Cala Moltó →

Cala Rajada

Cala Rajada was one of the first tourist centres in Mallorca. As the fishing and trading port of Capdepera, it still contains a certain charm. A ferry service connects Cala Rajada to Menorca.

Sa Torre Cega, a palace belonging to the powerful March family, stands out at the top of the hill overlooking the wharf. The palace itself cannot be visited but it is possible to see the gardens which are abundantly decorated with over sixty sculptural items by artists such as Henry Moore, Chillida, Rodin...

Lovely beaches include Cala Sa Font, Cala Agulla, a protected natural area, and Cala Mesquida.

Cala Moltó

Port of Cala Rajada

Canyamel / Coves d'Artà

The valley of Canyamel, a Natural Area of Special Interest due to its natural and scenic assets, extends along the course of the stream of the same name until reaching the well-known beaches. It gets its name from sugar cane growing (*canya de sucre* or *canyamel*), which began in 1468. Like the defence tower of Canyamel, the urbanisation was given the same name and built alongside the Caves of Artà, one of the most fascinating natural cavities that can be visited on the island.

As a curiosity, it should be mentioned that the sand on the beach had a decisive role in the fight against obesity. In the 1960s the workers from the Roche company who spent their summer holidays in the area had the curious habit of taking a fistful of sand away with them as a souvenir. An engineer from the company also took his fistful and analysed it: by pure coincidence he discovered a fungus, *streptomyces toxytricini*, an important ingredient in anti-obesity medicines.

Es Ribell beach

Cala de Canyamel

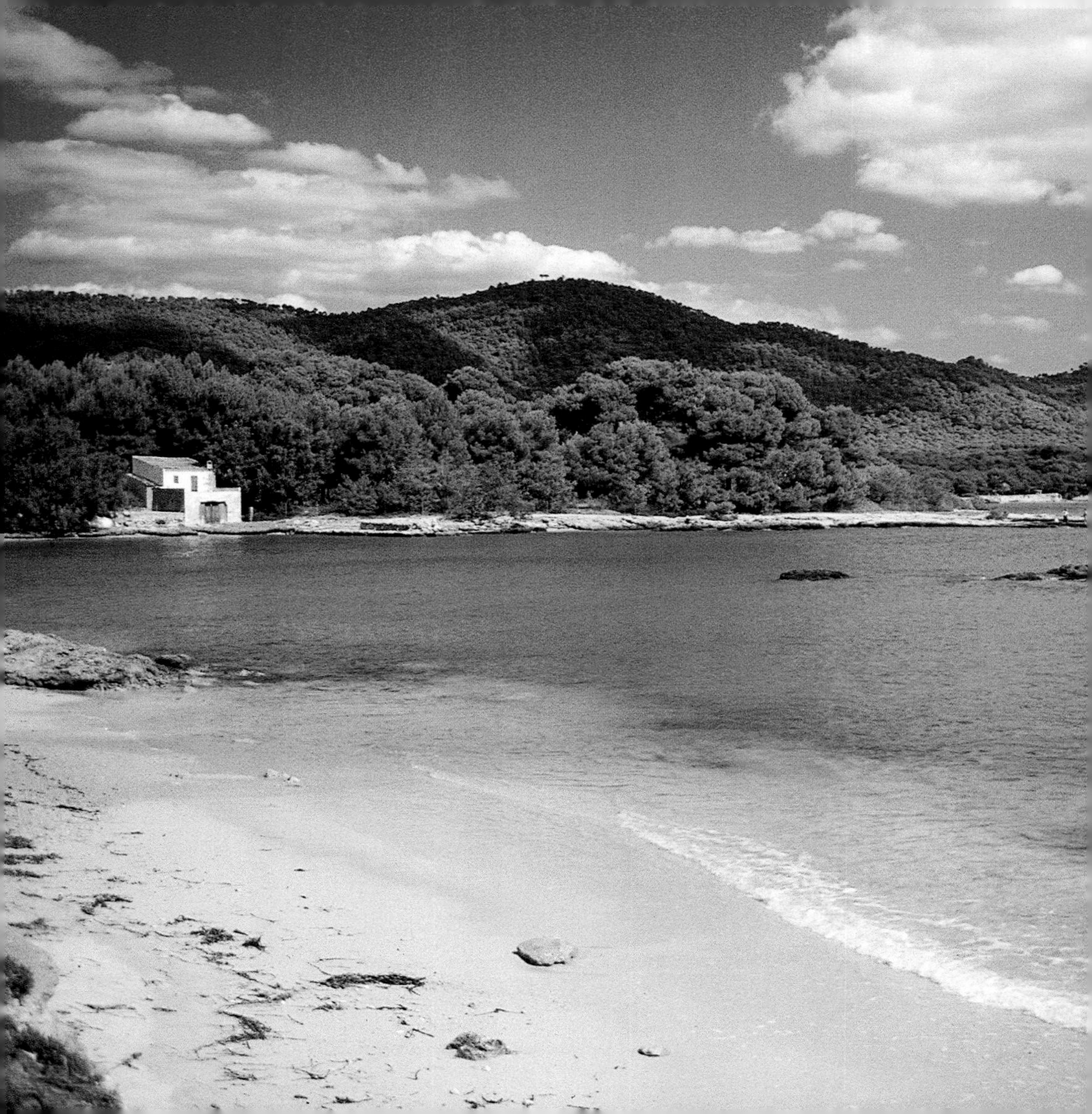

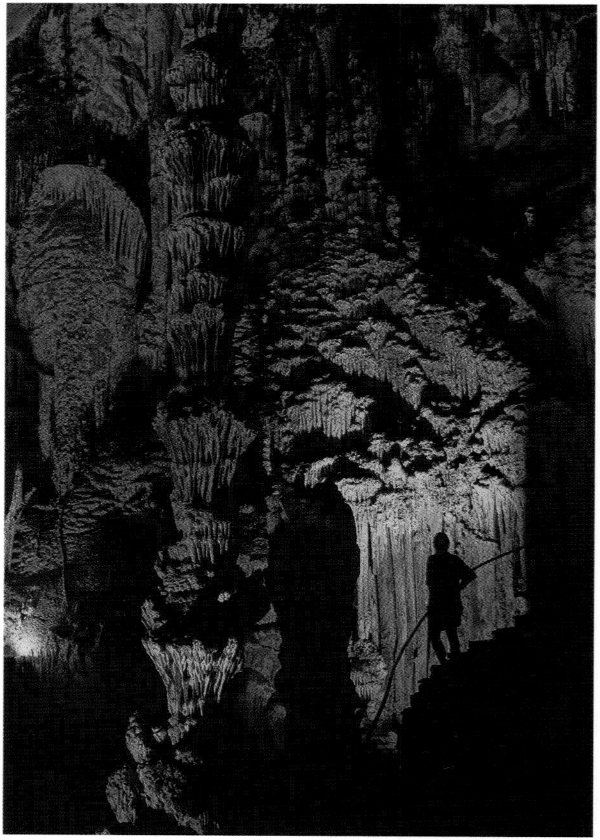

Interior of the caves of Artà

The entrance alone suggests a series of geological wonders →

Cala Bona / Cala Millor

Cala Bona is a small fishing port, which, despite its closeness to Cala Millor, has a more peaceful pace of life. The outskirts can also be a source of interesting trips and pleasant discoveries: Costa dels Pins, Son Servera, Sant Llorenç des Cardassar, S'Illot, with an interesting Talayotic settlement, Punta Amer, Natural Area of Special Interest where the 17th-century watchtower can be found and where today the well known Hot Air Balloon International Regatta is organised.

The beach of Cala Millor is over 2 km long and has an average width of 45 metres. Thanks to its fine sand and clear waters it has repeatedly been awarded the "blue flag" category of the European Community. The economic history of Cala Millor is in itself a brief summary of the history of tourism in Mallorca: it experienced the tourist development of the late-1960s and 70s, the crisis of the 80s and the improvement and sustainability plans of the 90s.

Son Servera sandy area

The explosion of flowers in spring spreads as far as the beaches

Portocristo

Portocristo is the port of Manacor and forms part of the municipality. Inhabited since prehistoric times, it was already an important enclave in the Roman period. The stream of Ses Talaioles has its outlet here, forming a beautiful channel in its final stretch. Around Portocristo are the Drac caves, along with the series of caves called Des Pirata and Dels Hams. The Drac caves feature the Martell lake, thought to be one of the largest underground lakes in the world; the Dels Hams caves house a curious life form: tiny crustaceans that have survived here since prehistoric times.

Manacor has a lot to offer in terms of cultural life. It is also where the famous Majorica pearls are produced (the factory can be visited). Other points of interest in the area include Cala Moreia, Cala Morlanda, Cala Petita, Cala Anguila, Cala Mendia, S'Estany d'en Mas, Cala Falcó and Cala Varques...

Sandy area inside the port

The port has given rise to a large tourist centre

One of the treasures of the Drac caves is the Martell lake

← The underground water reflects startling scenes

4
Cales de Mallorca
Portocolom
Santanyí
Colònia de Sant Jordi
Illa de Cabrera

Llucmajor
Felanitx
Cales de Mallorca
Cala Domingos
es Domingos
Santuari de Sant Salvador
510
Cala Murada
Cala Murada
Campos
Cas Concos des Cavallers
Castell de Santueri
Portocolom
Cala de s'Algar
s'Horta
Caló d'en Marçal
s'Alqueria Blanca
Calonge
Cala sa Nau
Cala Mitjana
ses Talaies de Can Jordi
sa Ràpita
Cala d'Or
es Salobrar de Campos
Santanyí
Marina de Cala d'Or
Platja de sa Ràpita
es Llombards
Parc Natural de Mondragó
Portopetro
ses Salines
Cala Mondragó
Platja des Trenc
Cala Santanyí
Cala Figuera
sa Colònia de Sant Jordi
Cala Llombards
es Pontàs
Cala Figuera
es Tamarells
Cala Santanyí
Cala Llombards
sa Talaia Grossa
Platja des Carbó
Estany de ses Gambes
Platja de ses Roquetes
Cala de S'Almunia
Cala en Tugores
Platja des Caragol
64
Cap de ses Salines
Freu de Cabrera
Illa des Conills
101
Parc Nacional de Cabrera
es Castell
146
172
Illa de Cabrera
N

Cales de Mallorca

Cales de Mallorca is a rather densely urbanised area that is mixed up with the urbanisations of Platja Tropicana, Cala Murada and Cala Antena, the whole area being full of beaches and small coves.

Between Manacor and Cales de Mallorca is the Torre dels Enagistes. It is an old defensive construction, dating from the 15th century, the inside of which has been fitted out as an archaeological and ethnological museum. Nearby is the district of Felanitx, with interesting smaller villages well worth visiting: Cas Concos des Cavaller, S'Horta, Es Carritxó, Son Mesquida, Son Negre, Son Valls...

Cala Magraner

Cala Es Domingos

Portocolom

Considered to be the port for the city of Felanitx, this is one of the largest natural ports on the island. It was from here that the wine and liquor produced in the area were loaded up for export to the continent, chiefly France, until, towards the end of the 19th century, the phylloxera plague destroyed the crops. Today, wine production is once again an important activity, after a long lapse in time, and it has an interesting aroma and taste.

The port was also the exciting setting of several episodes related to smuggling. Today, however, the old port lies dormant and its uses are much more leisurely.

Close to the port is Cala Marçal, a white sandy beach with all kinds of amenities. An interesting alternative to this one, quite close by, is the unspoilt cove of S'Algar.

Fishermen's port

Sa Capella

Almonds were once the sustenance of the Majorcan countryside
The harvesting is still done according to traditional methods →

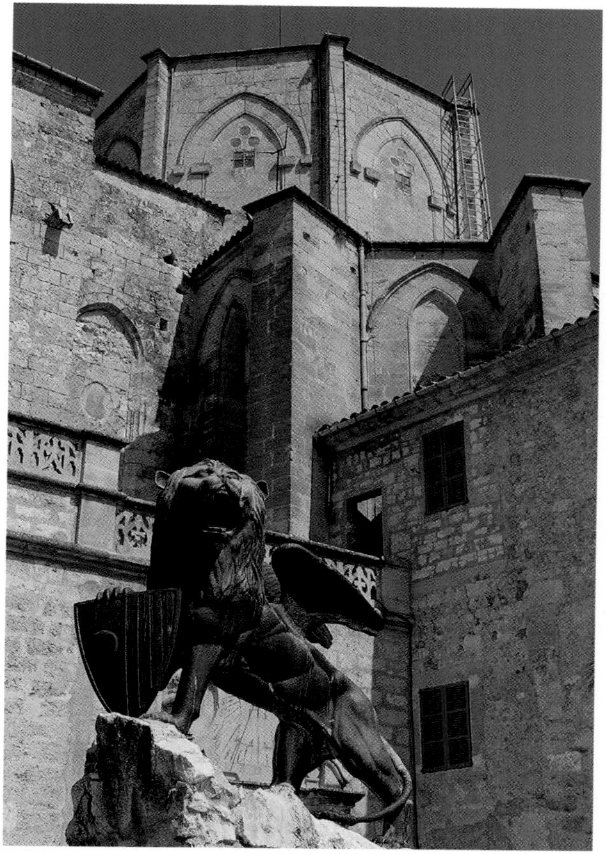

Sineu, in the centre of the island, is one of its historic towns

Coves of Montdragó and S'Amarador →→

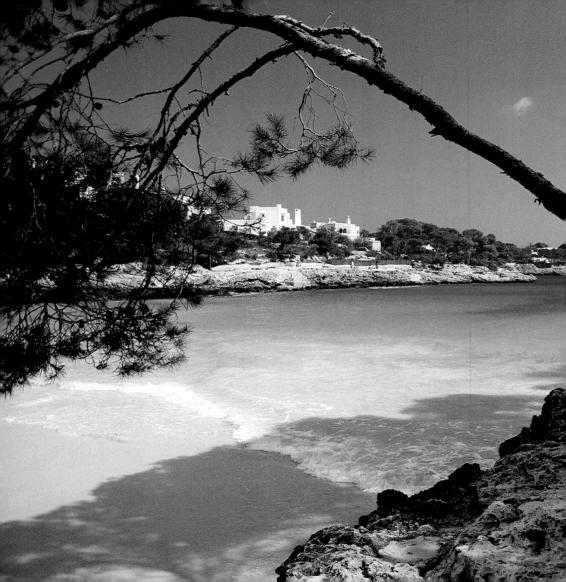

Cala d'Or

The atmosphere in Cala d'Or is pleasant and cosmopolitan. Around the three adjoining coves –Cala Llonga, Caló de ses Dones and Cala Gran– an enormous complex was constructed with a host of facilities and a marine port where exclusive, luxury yachts are moored. The centre is pedestrian-only and it has many attractive and sophisticated bars, shops and restaurants. Eating in one of the pleasant restaurants bordering the sea, or in the nautical club, is highly recommendable. Nearby Cala d'Or are Cala Esmeralda, Cala Ferrera and Cala de Sa Nau, beaches with fine sand and surrounded by pinewoods.

Turquoise-blue water in Cala Gran

Parking space for boats at sea level

Portopetro

Protecting the entrance to this deep port are the two points of Sa Torre and Es Frontet. It is an excellent shelter for sailors, however, with anchoring being much sought after and it is not easy to find a space. Since the 15th century it has been the exporting port of the famous Santanyí stone and of wheat.

Portopetro is a pleasant town in which the fishermen and the tourists mix together without either group disturbing the peace and beauty of the spot. The musician Frederic Mompou had his residence here.

Their quays provide sailors with an unbeatable shelter

Regatta inside the port

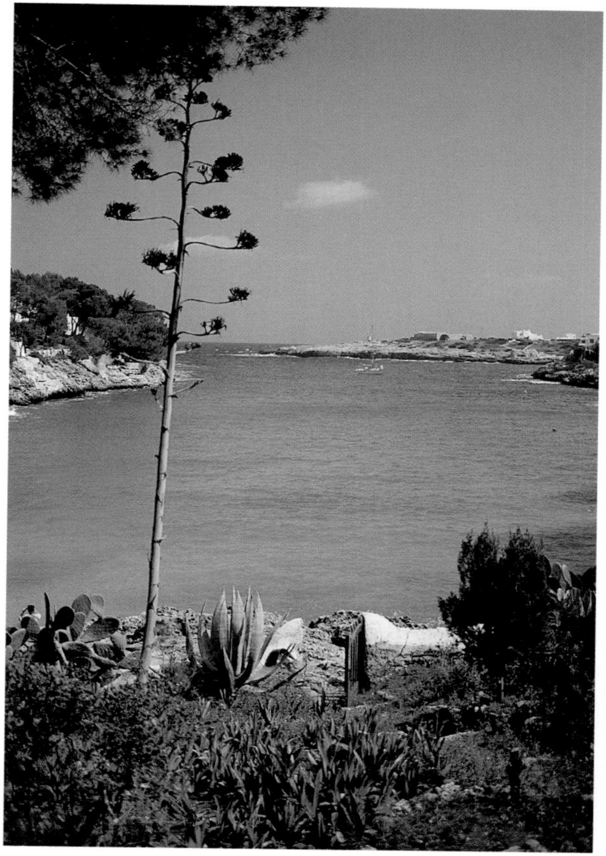

The irregular coastline hides paradisiacal scenery

← Peaceful small inlets were once the hiding spots for pirates

Cala Figuera

Cala Figuera is a natural shelter much appreciated by sailors visiting the island. In Cala Figuera you can wander around the port, which preserves an aesthetic air that speaks to us of bygone times, watch the fishermen repairing their nets, and understand why this spot is often chosen by home-based and international painters to reflect the beautiful serenity and peace that gently rock its waters.

Seafaring setting

The picturesque cove exudes calmness

LOS ANGELES

Santanyí

The name of this seven-hundred-year-old town, victim throughout history of different attacks and pirate incursions, comes from the Latin *Santi Agnini*. During the 19th century there was a mass migratory movement that took many of its inhabitants to the neighbouring island of Menorca, the coasts of Algeria and other towns in Mallorca. Tourism is the district's main activity, though there is some dry farming and quarries of *marès*, a sandstone of great fame on the island due to its amber colour. The district houses the vestiges of the prehistoric settlements of Sa Talaia Grossa and Ses Talaies de Can Jordi. It also has the Natural Park of Mondragó: a park of 785 ha., almost completely coastal, where there are a series of coves (S'Amarador, Caló del Brogit, Caló del Sivinar...) and cliffs that

Courtyard of Sa Rectoria

On Sundays there is a market in the square

reach a height of 30 metres (Cap del Moro, Solimina, El Blanquer...) The streams of the Amarador and the Coves del Rei form small ravines and flood areas that form more or less permanently filled lakes. A small strip of sand separates the lake from the sea on the beach of S'Amarador. It is an area with a wide range of settings (ravines, coves, dunes and marshland), resulting in a great variety of flora and fauna.

The town of Es Llombards, alongside the cove of the same name is well worth a visit. In Cala Llombards there is a spectacular stone arch carved out by the sea known as Es Pontàs. Other interesting spots are Cala S'Almoina and Cala Santanyí. The coastline that runs to Ses Salines is flat and open, but rises up to 64 metres at Cap de Ses Salines. This is the southernmost point of the island. The peacefulness and spectacular sight of its sunsets make this a very special place indeed.

Cala Santanyí possesses a beautiful beach

Es Pontàs

Cala S'Almonia, a local fishermen's shelter

← Inside the same cove

Caló des Moro, close to S'Almonia →→

Colònia de Sant Jordi

Colònia de Sant Jordi, whose seafront horizon is dominated by the silhouette of Cabrera, is considered as a family summer resort. Nearby are the sandy beaches of Carbó and Caragol. The coastline of Colònia de Sant Jordi features the islets of Na Guardis (an ancient Punic enclave that was a trading post), Caragol, Moltona and Pelada. There is also Es Trenc, a delightful dune beach and one of the few nudist beaches on the island. A short distance from this sandy area are the salt flats, exploited by the Romans, which form part of Salobrar de Campos, the second largest marshland area after S'Albufera. El Salobrar is a Bird Sanctuary (ZEPA).

Sports and fishing port

Seafront

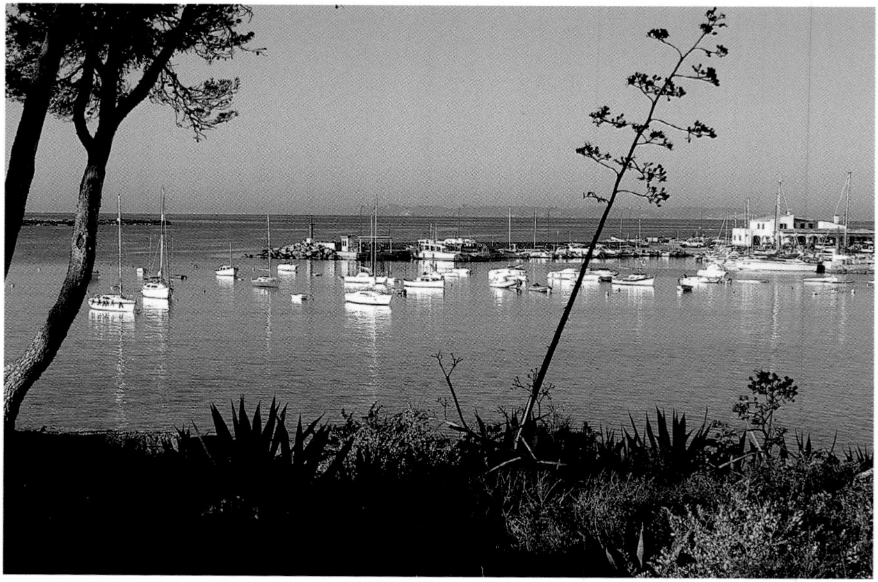

Colònia de Sant Jordi; detail of the port

Es Trenc beach, close to Ses Salines →

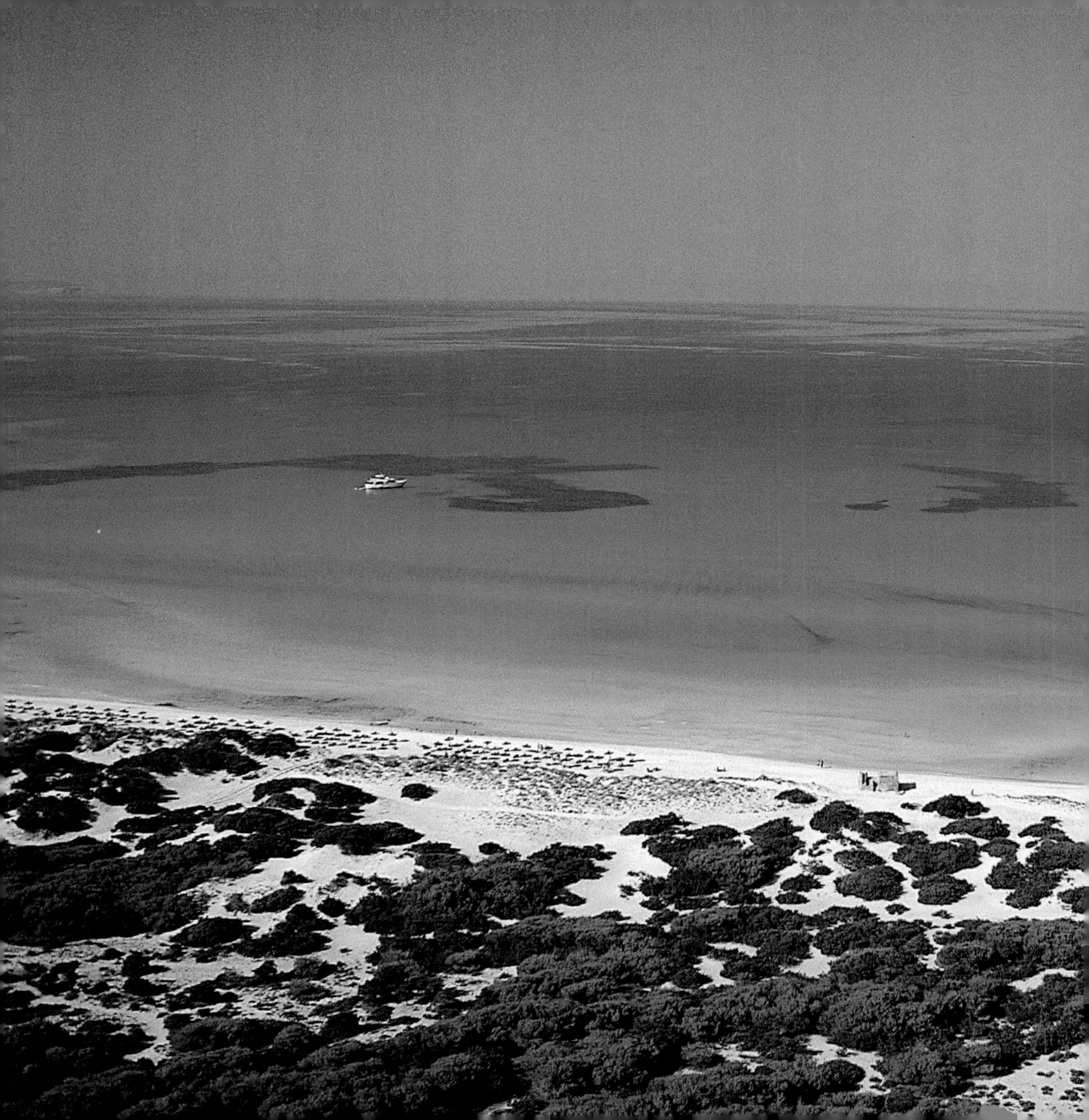

Illa de Cabrera

The archipelago of Cabrera, a national park of sea and land, is made up of the large islands of Cabrera and Illa de Conills as well as some 17 islets and reefs (na Pobra, na Foradada, na Plana, l'Esponja, na Rodona, els Estells, l'Imperial...). The landmass of the park covers 1,318 hectares, while the sea area is of 8,703 hectares. From the ports of Colònia de Sant Jordi, Portopetro or Sa Ràpita de Campos one can reach the park on a crossing that takes an hour and a half.

A token population has inhabited Cabrera throughout time, enabling the natural environment to be maintained completely intact. On reaching the island one catches sight of the 14th century castle, which from the top of a promontory overlooks the inlet of crystalline waters. A short distance from the port is a monolith that recalls the French soldiers who were confined, mistreated and abandoned here after the battle of Bailén.

The castle overlooks the port

Arriving on the island

© *Text*
ALBERT HERRANZ

© *Photographs*
JAUME SERRAT *Pages:* 9, 14, 24, 32-33, 39, 41, 42, 52, 58, 59, 66, 67, 68, 70, 72, 73, 74, 78, 80, 83 (1, 3), 85, 87, 88, 89, 90, 91, 93, 94, 101, 105, 106, 107, 111, 114, 115, 116, 118, 119, 120, 126-127, 130, 132, 138, 140, 145, 146, 150, 152, 158, 159, 161, 167, 174, 175, 177, 180, 181, 182-183, 185, 186, 187, 190, 191, 192, 193, 194, 195, 198-199, 200, 201, 202, 203, 204, 205 *and* 207 • **RICARD PLA** 27, 31, 38, 47, 48-49, 51, 57, 83 (4), 95, 103, 108, 113, 117 (3, 4), 123, 133, 134, 135, 153, 157, 162, 163, 176, 184, 188 *and* 189 • **SEBASTIÀ TORRENS** 53, 75, 102, 109, 112, 131, 136-137, 141, 142, 143, 149, 154 *and* 155 • **CARME VILA** 25, 37, 96, 97, 99, 100, 164, 165, 178, 179 *and* 196 • **MELBA LEVICK** 2, 15, 18, 55, 61, 71, 86 *and* 124 • **JORDI PUIG** 26, 46, 50, 83 (2), 92, 121, 151 *and* 156 • **SEBASTIÀ MAS** 12, 20, 23, 28, 45, 63 *and* 69 • **HUGO ARENELLA** 30, 40, 43, 54, 56, 84, 168 *and* 169 • **SERGI PADURA** 10-11, 21, 29, 35 *and* 144 • **JOAN MARC LINARES** 36, 64-65 *and* 81 • **BIEL SANTANDREU** 170 *and* 171 • **PERE VIVAS** 22 *and* 147 • **ANDRES CAMPOS** 60 *and* 62 • **JOAN OLIVA** 34 *and* 44 • **JOAN R. BONET** 98 *and* 197 • **AINA PLA** 117 (2) *and* 139 • **DANI CODINA** 122 *and* 125 • **MIGUEL RAURICH** 160 *and* 166 • **GASPAR VALERO** 79 • **ORIOL ALAMANY** 104 • **MIQUEL TRES** 82 •

Graphic design
MARTÍ ABRIL

Graphic edition
TRIANGLE POSTALS

Translation
STEVE CEDAR

Photomecanics
TECNOART

Printed by
NG NIVELL GRÀFIC
04-2006

Legally reg. B-9284-2004
ISBN 84-8478-072-4

TRIANGLE POSTALS
Sant Lluís, Menorca
Tel. 971 15 04 51
e-mail: triangle@infotelecom.es